Something Kindred

Something Kindred

by Nicole Tallman

Southern Collective Experience

www.southerncollectiveexperience.com

Copyright © 2022 by Nicole Tallman

All rights reserved. No part of this book may be reproduced or transmitted in any form or by any means, electronic or mechanical, including photocopying, recording, or any information storage and retrieval system, without permission in writing from the publisher.

ISBN: 978-1-7362306-1-9 – Paperback

Printed in the United States of America

This paper meets the requirements of ANSI/NISO Z39.48-1992 (Permanence of Paper)

Cover Design by Kaitlyn Young

Back Cover Headshot by Jackie Taylor

For my mother, Nancy, who was never ordinary, and for all the daughters and sons who are missing their mothers.

The death of a mother is the first sorrow wept without her.

-Anonymous

Contents

On The Last Moments Leading Up To Your Death..................3

On Surviving In The Early Days Following Your Death..................13

On Finding Your Ashes In My Suitcase..................23

On Reading Poems, I Now Sympathize
With Daughters Of Dead Mothers..................27

On Holidays After You're Gone..................31

On Sleeping On Your Pillow..................35

On Grieving..................39

On Love..................43

Acknowledgments..................47

Notes..................49

Praise For *Something Kindred*..................51

Foreword

Grief. It comes at you in so many forms it can be tougher to survive than loss itself. Sometimes it's as complicated as memory, others as blunt as a single note from a song.

Grief can pile itself at your feet like luggage that has to be toted a bit before it can be stored. To snatch it up and carry it, you have to have courage and strength, but those two will only take care of the lifting. If you want to make it through the storing, or the unpacking, you have to be as fluid and varied as grief is to manage its edges, its seams, its pockets, its weight.

Fluid. Varied. Strong. Courageous. I'd say these are all primary descriptors of Nicole Tallman's *Something Kindred*. Page by page, this book does the heavy lifting required to survive the loss of a loved one. Tallman fronts up to this loss without blinking. That's for sure. But this collection goes beyond all that to the necessary work of unpacking, of storing, of confession to clear all souls. And it's during those stages that grief can become slippery.

To manage all of grief's shapes and degrees, Tallman moves from the clinical directness of prose, to the hushed rasp of confession, and finally into crafted, curated lines of verse so she can make it through the complications of emotion, of memory, and of the future we all face day by day.

Ultimately, *Something Kindred* is a testament to the living, not the dying. To the lifting, the carrying, the unpacking, and the storing. This collection's pages are heavy, as is their burden. The kind of memories and experiences Tallman's grappling with here have mass and density. Real weight. But there is also hope and glory and deep breaths in these pages that give us the gift of clarity Tallman has earned.

Jack B. Bedell
Poet Laureate, State of Louisiana, 2017-2019
Author of *Color All Maps New*

Note to Reader

Dear Reader:

This is a chapbook of poems and prose for the grieving—not grieving in a rushed sense, but in a timeless sense. Because there is no real timeline that I've experienced. Grief is a messy, personal process. (More about that on page 39.)

After my mother died in 2017, I looked for a book of poems that would help me navigate my grief. I didn't find exactly what I was looking for... not because there aren't excellent books on the subject, but because I needed to write my own. The process of writing helped me process my feelings, and it is my hope that reading this chapbook will inspire you to write through your grief journey, no matter how busy your life may be. I'm still writing through my journey, sometimes in brief moments using the Notes app on my iPhone. I try to write at least a line every day, and I offer you, in the pages that follow, where my grief journey has taken me up to today.

When you feel hopeless, I hope you will come back to this page, know that there is someone who understands your grief, and that you find comfort in these words. I hope you will take the time you need to grieve, and I hope you will be inspired to write a line of poetry or a full poem to process how you feel. If you'd like, you can share your poems with me at nicoleatallman@gmail.com. I will read them, and I will send you love and light.

With gratitude,

Nicole Tallman

Miami, Florida
January 22, 2022 (the fifth anniversary of my mother's death)

By the time I arrive in Cheboygan from Miami, you are not very lucid. Your death bed is in the game room—a fitting Michigan death among the deer heads. You get so excited to see me that your eyes get big like a child's and you gasp as you look at your sister. Like you've seen an angel. You tell me you waited for me. I say I hurried. You ask how the speech was. It's the evening after the State of the County. It's the first one you didn't watch via livestream. I say it was fine. You say you are too.

On The Last Moments Leading Up To Your Death

It's the only time I see Dad cry in 40 years. He says you'll be gone in three days. I ask why he didn't tell me sooner. He says he didn't know it would happen so fast. There were signs we didn't see, but you had said you'd let me know when to come home. You did, and I don't blame you. You couldn't know what you didn't want to know. You just kept pretending, even from the Hospice bed at home. How could I be surprised that you would pretend that everything was fine? Your entire life was pretending, making everyone believe that everything was fine.

The Hospice nurse's name is Natalie. She hands me a book to prepare me for your death. She tells me it won't be long.

You want to get up to use the bathroom. Dad and I take you there. You worry that your hands are dirty. I wash them with a wipe. You thank me with a voice too small for your body.

At some point, you stop asking for food. I ask if you will eat something for me. You ask for a cherry popsicle. And when it hits your lips, you slurp it loud, like a hungry little bird. When you don't finish your popsicle, I ask to feed you. Dad hands me the dropper of morphine. It's like caring for a baby. I measure everything so carefully. Record it. It gets more difficult as you get closer to the end. Your mouth more rigid. Your eyes rolling back in your head. There's no dignity in dying this way.

Natalie comes to give you a final bath. To drain your ascites. She speaks to you like an adult child. The smell coming out of you is metal. It's the sign of a failing liver. I keeping smelling your head to try to recognize you. Natalie and I change your clothes and dress you in your favorite pajamas. I rub lotion on your feet and put warm, fuzzy socks on them. I worry that your toenails are too long, but don't want to hurt you by trimming them. I don't want you to have to wear a diaper, but Natalie says you have to. You ask to get up again to go to the bathroom. I tell you Natalie says you have to stay in bed. You nod and concede. I bring you a stuffed bear for comfort, but you don't want it anymore.

You die around 4:44 p.m. There are four of us in the room: Dad, your twin sisters, and me. It's too much for your mother, and I've asked the others to give us space. It's too many people for you to let go of. And I know who you really want there. Your heart is strong so it takes long for your body to go. I try walking away to see if that might help you transition. You hold on. I hold your feet at the end of the bed. It isn't until I whisper in your ear, *Thank you for being such a good mother to me. I love you. You can go now.* that you finally let yourself go. I count every one of your breaths. Watch the slower and slower rise and fall of your chest. The rattle of each last breath. Until Dad tells me that's it. I look at the clock. Then I text Natalie to let her know you're gone.

Confession: I took several photos of you as you were dying. In our moments alone. I keep the photos on my phone. I show them to no one. When you were dead, I waited until everyone left the room, and then I took several more. For myself. I never saw you so still. I didn't want to forget the look of peace on your face.

On Surviving In The Early Days Following Your Death

I sleep on the couch, swaddled in your blanket, in the sunroom because I can't fall asleep in my bed. I take a Klonopin and try to see you in the stars through the skylight, but it's covered in snow. When I doze off, you wake me up with electricity. The zap of your energy leaving the house kills the microwave. The night of the day you died, so did the microwave.

Dad gets up. Checks the activities off his daily to-do list as he does them. Makes coffee, oatmeal, and fruit. We make a new grocery list together. At the top, a new microwave. He's no good on the stove. I walk over to look at your stove. There's a chip missing. I ask what happened. He said you dropped something...that your hands got clumsy because of the neuropathy. I'm surprised you allowed the imperfection to stay on the stove. I cover the chipped paint instinctively with my finger, then Dad and I go to the store to pick out a new microwave.

The cat is confused. He stays awake all day. Crouches down low, cries out, loud and strangled. Swats at nothing. Paces like an orphan. Sits down in a spot somewhere near where your death bed used to be. Coughs up a hair ball. I tell Dad it's time to get the carpet cleaned.

You said you didn't want a funeral, so we cremate you I don't know where, but I hear something about a cement yard. I write your obituary. Realize there's a lot I don't know about you. Dad and I pick out urns to divide you into. I give the largest part of you to Dad in a big silver urn. I divide the rest among your twin sisters and myself. I don't portion out any for your mother. Grandma says she should have gone first. I don't disagree with her. Dad says he should have gone first too. I don't disagree with him either.

Dad and I take a trip in the snow to get the rings you left me resized. Dad also asks me if he should take off his wedding ring. He isn't sure of the proper thing to do. I tell him not to worry about what's proper. He should just do what feels right. He isn't sure what to do with that. He says 45 years of marriage is a long time.

I need to get back to Miami. Someone tells me life goes on. I pack as much of you with me as I can. I take your last hat, gloves, and scarf. I take some of your pills. I take one of your wigs. I take your last purse. I take the jewelry and clothes you set aside for me. I take a lock of the little of your hair that remained—the lock I cut off your head at the funeral home. I take your communion bible. I take pictures of your cleaning instructions and your shopping lists. I take pictures of the pictures in your albums. I wash a pair of your Hello Kitty pajamas and drop them off at Hospice to have a memory bear made out of them.

Confession: On the plane ride home, I wear your clothes. I say little mantras to keep from crying. I drink a beer with someone else's mother.

On Finding Your Ashes In My Suitcase

I think you would laugh if I told you,
your urn exploded somewhere
during my flight back to Miami.

And when I got home, I found you spilled
your ashes all over the inside of my luggage.
Actually, it was your luggage—

the Liz Claiborne zebra print carry-on
with the dragon fruit interior.
The flight was oversold, so I was forced

to check you in your luggage.
What kind of monster
makes a grieving daughter check her own mother?

Confession: I find myself obsessively Google searching ways to cope with the death of one's mother. I discover Sylvia Plath's daughter Frieda Hughes, a poet and painter.

On Reading Poems, I Now Sympathize With Daughters Of Dead Mothers

-For Frieda Hughes

It's hard to look at this picture of Frieda and not feel something tragic—
mother, father, brother dead,
one by oven, one by cancer, one by hanging.

It's hard just to look at this picture of Frieda, with her menagerie
of pets, poems, and paintings.
Yes, I mean the Frieda with an e,

not Frida Kahlo.
Frieda Hughes, I want to buy one of your paintings

a green one
*representing the joy of being able to work on my poetry
or something other creative.*

Frieda Hughes, I want to eat all of your mother's poems
and all of your paintings.

It's hard not to look at Frieda and feel
something kindred—
us daughters of dead mothers.

It's hard to look at Frieda and feel
something so protective,
to say to us through our mothers

There, there. You made it.

Confession: On our first Christmas without you, Dad doesn't decorate the tree. He buys a small tabletop one from Pier One Imports. I think of all the care and effort you used to put into decorating for the holidays. Dad and I are too sad to put in that much effort.

On Holidays After You're Gone

Missing
you on Christmas

missing you in your house
missing you on Lake Michigan

missing you, who said you'd be around forever
not dead when I was 40

missing you, who I can still see in the reflection
of my eyes in the water

and in the halo
of the pink sky at night

missing the way
you'd say sailor's delight

missing you
in the sunrise and the sunset, and every

moment in between
in God's bowling thunder

in a leopard print shirt
in almost everything

Always missing you
my heart is now 40 floors up in my body

Confession: Your sister-in-law told me you would visit me one night... that you would come to me in my dreams or when I least expect it. To facilitate the connection, I sleep on the pillow you used to sleep on when you would visit me in Miami.

On Sleeping On Your Pillow

Every night I sleep on your old pillow
even though it's yellowed with time.
It's not an ugly yellow.
It's yellow like the crocuses
and the daffodils I'd pick for you
because you'd refuse store-bought flowers.

You know yellow used to be my least favorite color—
the color of teeth tinged with age,
the color of fingers stained with nicotine,
the color of infection and fangled sunflowers.
Did you know there's a word for fear of sunflowers?
It's helianthophobia.

But now there's a nostalgia I feel with certain shades of yellow—
the dandelion yellow of your failed liver,
the canary yellow of the beanie you wore on your balding, dying head,
the mustard yellow of the last purse you bought,
the marigold in the memory of your small yellow hand,
I held it until you said, *You've got to stop touching me so much.*

Confession: I never imagined the loneliness of grieving a loss without you.

On Grieving

Confession: When I miss you, I reread the note and the poem you left for me in the safe. I try to find the joy in being alive. I try to remember and reclaim what I love.

On Love

-       *After Alex Dimitrov*

I love morning before I've used my voice.

I love morning before anyone has spoken.

I love Miami in February.

I love the word petrichor.

I love the smell of petrichor.

I love velvet blazers and wearing them despite the weather and occasion.

I love buying myself red roses.

I love drinking rose water.

I love Chartreuse, Champagne, and Chambord.

I love the way that sounds.

I love finding books with old notes hidden between the pages.

I love that my cat looks annoyed when I come home from work.

I love that my partner looks happy when I come home from work.

I love deep conversations with people I'll never see again.

I love the moon more than the sun.

I love Medusa and her head of snakes.

I love drawing the Hermit card from the Tarot deck.

I love my Salvador Dalí Tarot deck.

I love being alone in the forest.

I love being alone in a field of lavender.

I love being alone without feeling lonely.

I love being an only child.

I love that happy hour isn't always happy.

I love not owning a home.

I love wooden matches.

I love candles with wooden wicks that crackle.

I love a wood-burning fire.

I love people who own fireplaces in Miami.

I love that a Miami summer can feel more brutal than a Michigan winter.

I love going to the beach when there's no sun.

I love a well-made bed and a well-ironed shirt.

I love the occasional earworm.

I love tuning everything out.

I love people who aren't afraid to say no.

I love holding the door open for others.

I love changing my mind.

I love squirrels that store food for the winter.

I love food made with love.

I love birds that don't fly south for the winter.

I love a conspiracy of ravens.

I love the seagull I once saw eating a discarded orange.

I love a peacock presenting its colors.

I love a flamingo standing on one leg.

I love the angels that adults leave in the first snow that sticks.

I love early spring crocuses as they push through the snow.

I love anatomical drawings of the human heart.

I love the idea of touring every abandoned asylum.

I love that this experience is likely better in my head than it would be in reality.

I love frogs croaking in summer ponds.

I love paddle boating around lily pads.

I love when the muses speak to me.

I love the highest note on the violin.

I love the French who don't like me.

I love wearing my mother's clothes.

I love landing in a city I've never been before.

I love returning to a city I've loved before.

I love train rides through the country.

I love ladybugs that don't act like proper ladies.

I love deer that make it to the other side of the road.

I love the idea that everything really works out in the end.

I love a day with no social events.

I love you for reading this poem.

Acknowledgments

First, my love and gratitude to my amazing partner, Militza. My thanks to my father, Dale, who says he doesn't understand poetry, but listens to mine nonetheless. To my Aunts Diane and Jaki who have become second mothers to me, along with my Miami mother, Yelitza. To my Uncle Paul and cousins Natasha and Mikey, who mean the world to me. To all of my childhood friends who have become lifelong friends, but especially Amy (Jackson) Greene and Autumn (Anderson) Gardner. To my core "France" crew: Wallace Holder, Jennifer Waldner, and Peter Woodhouse, and to the amazing category-defying Dan Poskey, Mary Mumper, Lela Boswell, and Sentil (BeeJay) Balaji. To all of my elementary, middle and high school teachers, along with my college professors from Grand Valley State University and the University of Central Florida. I love and respect you all.

My heartfelt gratitude to Clifford Brooks III for publishing "On Reading Poems, I Now Sympathize With Daughters of Dead Mothers" and "On Grieving" in the February 2021 issue of *The Blue Mountain Review*, for welcoming me to The Southern Collective Experience, and for taking a chance on this chapbook. I also want to thank J. Archer Avary for publishing "On Finding Your Ashes In My Suitcase" and "On Sleeping On Your Pillow" in *Sledgehammer Lit*.

My thanks to Kaitlyn Young for the gorgeous cover design and to Jackie Taylor for the magical headshot.

My sincere thanks and appreciation to the following poets and editors for their insight, feedback and encouragement on the poems that make up this chapbook: Jack Bedell, Maureen Seaton, Richard Blanco, Dorothea Lasky, Alex Dimitrov and fellow poets from Hudson Valley Writers Center, Amelia Martens, Jared Beloff (especially for helping me with the title), Jenny Xu, and my fellow editors from *South Florida Poetry Journal*, especially Lenny DellaRocca.

My thanks and gratitude to the Mayor of Miami-Dade County Daniella Levine Cava—a tremendous supporter of the arts—who has given me the honor of serving as her Poetry Ambassador, and to my entire Miami-Dade County family.

My thanks to The Center for Writing and Literature at Miami Dade College, along with the Miami Book Fair, and to the writing friends, teachers, and mentors I've met along the way: Melissa Burley, Roxanna Elden, Carol Sue Gershman, Gariot Louima, Ana Martinez Orizondo, Lissette Mendez, and Natalia Sylvester.

And finally, to you, my dear readers. It all starts and ends with you. Thank you so much for taking the time to read this chapbook and for your support of the written word when there are so many competing choices for your time and attention.

Notes

The cover photo for this book was taken by my mother, Nancy, and I credit her posthumously.

The introductory text on page 7 and the confessions throughout this chapbook represent a continuing dialogue with my mother, as do all of the poems except "On Reading Poems, I Now Sympathize With Dead Daughters," "On Grieving", and "On Love."

The italicized line in "On Reading Poems, I Now Sympathize With Dead Daughters" is borrowed from Frieda Hughes' website and the poem is dedicated to her.

"On Grieving" was written in response to the Kübler-Ross model of grief, which attempted to "normalize" grief. As I navigated the death of my mother, I started to see grief not as something that was happening in five or seven stages that I was entering and exiting, but as a blurry, imperfect circle of alternating distraction and reflection activities. I liken grief more to Ouroboros eating his own tail—to the idea that we (or parts of ourselves) may need to vanish from view from time to time to keep existing...that we may need to deconstruct or kill off parts of our old self to recreate a new self that allows us to carry on after our losses.

"On Love" is styled after Alex Dimitrov's endless poem "Love," which you can find by visiting @apoemcalledlove on Twitter.

Praise For *Something Kindred*

Something Kindred is a testament to the living, not the dying. To the lifting, the carrying, the unpacking, and the storing. This collection's pages are heavy, as is their burden. The kind of memories and experiences Nicole Tallman's grappling with here have mass and density. Real weight. But there is also hope and glory and deep breaths in these pages that give us the gift of clarity Tallman has earned.

JACK B. BEDELL, Poet Laureate, State of Louisiana, 2017-2019, Author of *Color All Maps New*

Through the spare beauty of haiku and the fineness of *belles-lettres*, Nicole Tallman pens an evocative and stirring account of grieving that echoes with ache in our hearts, but also soothes us with the understanding that love is immortal despite our losses.

RICHARD BLANCO, 2013 Presidential Inaugural Poet

Nicole Tallman's *Something Kindred* grapples with the big loss—that of a mother. Tallman meticulously details her mother's passing including taking photographs of her mother meant "only for her" and Hello Kitty pajamas. Confessional and celebratory, these prose poems and vignettes (and an inventive "circle" poem!) dare to grieve and dare to live beyond death.

DENISE DUHAMEL, Author of *Second Story*, *Scald*, and *Blowout* (finalist for the National Book Critics Circle Award)

Grief, the brutal blessing of it, has the strength to wake us and the power to keep us secret from ourselves. In *Something Kindred,* Nicole Tallman chooses to waken. In stark, declarative sentences and spare, unflinching lines, she navigates a path into a daughter's grief—*into* it. So often, in our fast-paced world of commodifications and immediate gratifications, we wish to move *through* things, to find the takeaway, to be done with troubles before they begin. But Nicole Tallman understands that the great labor is to go into the mysteries, to let them do their work, to let them shake us until we are truly here. «I love food made with love,» she writes. And the feast of *Something Kindred*, bitter as its griefs may be, is made with enough love to bring us to each other. Until being here together is enough.

JOSEPH FASANO, Author of *The Dark Wild Heart of Everything* and *The Crossing*

In *Something Kindred*, we find a touching tribute from a grateful daughter to a resilient mother gone too soon. We witness a visceral hole expanding in the hearts of her loved ones, as she fades away like an autumnal sunset. Importantly, we also see the strength, solemnity of Michigan winters in a mother's soldiering on until the last moment; that famous Midwestern resolve, for her family. Ultimately, this is a serene collection about a daughter holding onto her mother, this book, a fitting homage to pure love.

JOSE HERNANDEZ DIAZ, Author of *The Fire Eater*

Nicole Tallman's stunning and emotional collection, *Something Kindred*, contains the poems that make us feel less alone. Poignant, honest, powerful, vulnerable, these poems broke me open in the best way. From a series of "confessions" to "On Reading Poems, I Now Sympathize With Daughters Of Dead Mothers," this book takes us on a journey where an urn must be checked and not carried on an airplane to *now there's a nostalgia I feel with certain shades of yellow*. Tallman is a generous poet who took her grief and created a book to help us with ours, but also, to remind us to live and love hard. This was a book I could not set down until I read the final thoughtful, beautiful poem. This book is a gift.

KELLI RUSSELL AGODON, Author of *Dialogues with Rising Tides*

Something Kindred is a fearless, achingly honest, absolutely gorgeous and essential poetic sequence on grief for all of us who have lost a loved one. I needed this book. Now more than ever, it's true, when it seems there is not enough time to grieve those I/we have lost. But this little book is timeless. And universal. Tallman's poems and prose embody the very words our hearts hold close. Kindred, indeed: clan, tribe, house, ally, flesh and blood. In *Something Kindred*, Nicole Tallman has found a way to connect us all.

MAUREEN SEATON, Author of *Undersea* and *Sweet World* (winner of the Florida Book Award)

Like the inside of a magician's hat, *Something Kindred holds* much more than seems physically possible from an outside glance: an entire mother who must be divided into urns; a grief seemingly too large to fit into a mere human body; and the entire psychology of loss and loneliness delivered by aphorism, like a spinning world stabilized on the head of a pin. Beautiful, resilient, and true, these poetic offerings remind us that, yes, sometimes what we love will vanish, but we are the real magicians. We are the ones with the power to carry, within ourselves, everything we don't want to lose.

MELISSA STUDDARD, Author of *I Ate the Cosmos for Breakfast*

Nicole Tallman serves as the Poetry Ambassador for Miami-Dade County Mayor Daniella Levine Cava, an Associate Editor for *South Florida Poetry Journal* and Interviews Editor for *The Blue Mountain Review*.

Find her on Twitter and Instagram @natallman

and at www.nicoletallman.com.

www.ingramcontent.com/pod-product-compliance
Lightning Source LLC
Chambersburg PA
CBHW072209100526
44589CB00015B/2439